American pop culture

Television and Movies

Philip Abraham

Children's Press®
A Division of Scholastic Inc.
New York / Toronto / London / Auckland / Sydney
Mexico City / New Delhi / Hong Kong
Danbury, Connecticut

Book Design: Mindy Liu and Michael DeLisio
Contributing Editor: Shira Laskin
Photo Credits: Cover © Columbia Pictures/courtesy Everett Collection;
p. 4 © Digital Vision/Getty Images; p. 7 © Getty Images; pp. 8, 10 © Corbis;
p. 13 © Hulton-Deutsch Collection/Corbis; pp. 15, 21, 22, 31 © Bettmann/Corbis;
p. 16 © John Springer Collection/Corbis; p. 24 © Hulton/Archive/Getty Images;
p. 27 © Wally McNamee/Corbis; p. 28 © Globe Photos, Inc.; p. 33 © AFP/Corbis;
pp. 34, 41 courtesy Everett Collection; p. 36 © Neal Preston/Corbis; p. 39
© Reuters NewMedia Inc./Corbis

Library of Congress Cataloging-in-Publication Data

Abraham, Philip, 1970-
    Television and movies / Philip Abraham.
    p. cm.—(American pop culture)
    Summary: An overview of movies and television in America, in the context
of popular culture, from the late nineteenth century until today.
    Includes bibliographical references and index.
    ISBN 0-516-24074-9 (lib. bdg.) — ISBN 0-516-25946-6 (pbk.)
    1. Motion pictures—Juvenile literature. 2. Television
broadcasting—Juvenile literature. [1. Motion pictures. 2. Television
broadcasting. 3. Popular culture—United States.] I. Title. II. Series.

PN1994.A5227 2004
791.43'0973—dc22

                                            2003015394

1 2 3 4 5 6 7 8 9 10 R 13 12 11 10 09 08 07 06 05 04

Contents

Spending time watching television with friends has become a favorite American pastime.

Introduction

It is Saturday evening. You and your friend are trying to figure out what to do tonight. Should you go to the movies or stay home and watch your favorite TV shows? The movie you want to see got great reviews and your friends loved it. You are tempted to go, but you have been waiting all week to see what will happen next on your favorite TV shows. Should you choose the thrill of a great film? Or should you choose the comfort of spending a few hours with the TV characters you love?

Movies and television are a very special part of American pop culture. Since each was developed, what we've seen on the big and small screens have reflected and helped to shape American society. Movies and television represent and define mainstream American culture.

Over the years, movies and TV shows have been true signs of the times. Each has offered heroes and role models to an ever-changing America. They have helped us through troubled years, brought important historical events into our homes, and communicated what it means to be an American at any point in history. We love to watch because we feel connected to the images we see. TV shows and movies that celebrate the American spirit have found places in our hearts—and at the core of American pop culture.

In 2001, Americans spent over $8 billion on movie tickets.

Eadweard Muybridge's early photographs of animals and people in motion helped create the motion picture industry.

Early Movies and Television

Capturing Motion

In the late 1870s, Eadweard Muybridge paved the way for modern movies when he succeeded in photographing motion. Muybridge was a British inventor working in California. He took a set of photographs of a running horse by lining up a row of cameras with strings attached to them. As the horse raced past each string, it triggered the cameras. Muybridge ended up with a series of photos that showed an unbroken line of motion. His success inspired other inventors to come up with ways to record moving images.

Fred Ott's Sneeze, created in 1894, was one of Thomas Edison's earliest films. It features Fred Ott, an Edison employee, sneezing comically for the camera. The film was the first motion picture to be copyrighted in the United States. This protected the film from being copied or sold by anyone other than Edison.

In the late 1880s, Thomas Edison became involved in similar work. He asked his assistants to work on developing this technology. One of his workers, William K. L. Dickson, developed the kinetograph. This was a special camera that could record moving images on film. Dickson also invented a separate machine, called a kinetoscope, that allowed people to see the recorded images. The kinetoscope had a peephole through which a person could watch very short silent films. The films were a hit, and kinetoscope parlors opened in many cities in the United States.

By the early 1900s, new motion picture cameras had been developed. With them came a machine that changed the industry—the projector. Projectors used light to show film

Did You Know ?

AROUND 1905, THOUSANDS OF MOVIE THEATERS CALLED NICKELODEONS OPENED ACROSS AMERICA. THEY WERE CALLED NICKELODEONS BECAUSE IT COST A NICKEL FOR A TICKET.

images on a screen. People no longer had to wait for a turn to see a movie through the peephole of a kinetoscope. They could now go to a theater and watch a film with many others.

As movie-watching became a shared experience, movie theaters replaced kinetoscope parlors across the nation. One of the most famous films of this time was *The Great Train Robbery* (1903). The 10-minute film showed a train being robbed followed by the chase and capture of the criminals involved. Audiences loved it.

Hooray for Hollywood!

During the early years of moviemaking, most filmmakers and studios were located on the East Coast of the United States, in New York City and New Jersey. By 1914, however, many movie companies had moved to Hollywood, in southern California. Hollywood offered moviemakers good year-round weather as well as different settings, such as beaches, mountains, and deserts.

The Great Train Robbery was directed by Edwin S. Porter and filmed on location on the Lackawanna Railroad in New Jersey.

Sound Enters the Picture

The Jazz Singer, made in 1927, was the first full-length movie to feature sound. The sound was provided by a disk that was played at the same time as the movie. The disk had to be started at the same time as the movie in order to match the sound to the images onscreen. Within a few years, the technology changed and most movies were made with sound electronically encoded in the film.

King's Ridge Christian School
Media Center

Inventing the Television

Like movies, the birth of television can be traced back to the 1800s. Many scientists and inventors contributed ideas that created a foundation for modern television. The first was Paul Gottlieb Nipkow, a German inventor who created the Nipkow Disk in 1884. The disk was the first machine to send pictures over short distances through wires.

In 1923, Vladimir Zworykin invented a special television camera tube called the iconoscope. He also invented a picture tube used to show the images the iconoscope recorded. Many other inventions around the globe led to experimental television broadcasts in the late 1920s and 1930s.

In 1936, the Radio Corporation of America (RCA) teamed with Zworykin to place television sets in 150 homes in the New York City area. The team then began sending out experimental TV broadcasts from the Empire State Building to these homes. The efforts were successful. RCA began regular broadcasting as the National Broadcasting Company (NBC).

The 1939 New York World's Fair was home to the first televised presidential address. Viewers watched as President Franklin D. Roosevelt announced the opening of the fair.

On April 30, 1939, the opening of the 1939 New York World's Fair was broadcast over the air. RCA used the World's Fair to promote the sale of their TV sets. Most sets were 5 by 12 inches (12.7 by 25.4 centimeters) and sold for between $200 and $600. Two years later, the United States entered World War II. The American public would have to wait a few years for television to become a part of everyday life.

15

Audiences identified with movie characters' intense feelings in war-time films, such as *Casablanca*, in 1942.

Movies and Television in the War Years

As America entered the war, television's development was put on hold. The materials needed to make TV sets were needed for the war effort. The technical and business people involved in the TV industry also helped. They turned their attention toward making equipment to help the United States' military fight the war.

Movies Go to War

Movies, however, played an important role during the war. People wanted to escape their stress and fears about the war. Moviemakers saw that films could inspire Americans to feel hopeful about life again. Members of the movie industry also banded together to help serve their country through their art. Movies educated Americans about the war. They explained who Americans were fighting and why.

Movies also expressed an important government message to the public: Americans needed to make sacrifices in their daily lives to help the war effort overseas. No movie showed this better than *Casablanca*.

Humphrey Bogart and Ingrid Bergman starred as a couple torn between their love for one another and their duty to serve America. Americans related to the characters' feelings. They felt scared, hurt, passionate, and hopeful along with the actors onscreen. Since the movie's characters were in the same situation as Americans, American viewers immediately felt connected to the story. Bogart and Bergman didn't come across as actors on a screen. Their portrayals were so true to life, they felt more like friends or neighbors.

The War Ends and TV Takes Off
Shortly after the end of World War II, TV programs were on the air again. By 1947,

there were twelve TV stations broadcasting to about 14,000 homes across America. As sales of TV sets increased, advertisers began to see television as a great way to inform customers about their products. Soon advertisers were sponsoring, or paying for, shows that would allow them to advertise their products during breaks in the programming.

One of the first successful sponsored shows was *Texaco Star Theater*. Hosted by Milton Berle, the show featured a variety of entertaining acts, such as comedy skits and

Did You Know ?

MANY AMERICAN MOVIE STARS, INCLUDING BOB HOPE, TRAVELED OVERSEAS TO ENTERTAIN TROOPS INVOLVED IN WWII. THE STARS BECAME SYMBOLS OF AMERICAN VALUES, REMINDING THE TROOPS TO KEEP THE AMERICAN SPIRIT OF FREEDOM ALIVE. OTHER MOVIE STARS, SUCH AS THE COMEDY TEAM OF ABBOTT AND COSTELLO, TOURED WITHIN THE UNITED STATES. THEY URGED AMERICANS TO BUY WAR BONDS. WAR BONDS WERE A WAY FOR THE AMERICAN PUBLIC TO HELP THE GOVERNMENT PAY FOR THE EXPENSIVE WAR EFFORT.

musical guests. It was a huge hit. Berle became one of television's first celebrities. He became so popular that many Americans went out to buy TV sets just to be able to watch his show.

Milton Berle introduced America to the power of a TV celebrity. His friendly charm made Americans feel comfortable and happy. Many of his viewers stopped doing their normal chores just to watch his show. Businesses even reported that fewer customers came in to their stores while the show was on the air.

Watching Berle became a shared American experience. A person sitting at home on a Tuesday night enjoying the show knew that his friends and neighbors were doing the same in their own homes. The show provided Americans with a common bond, bringing them together in a new way. Even though they weren't sitting in a room together, they were sharing the joy of watching together. Americans had a taste of the magic of television—and they were ready for more.

American TV audiences fell in love with Milton Berle. Often called "Uncle Miltie," Berle was considered a member of every American family.

New Programs

As television continued to gain popularity, TV networks began to create different kinds of programs. The new shows included situation comedies (sitcoms), dramas, Westerns, game shows, and children's programs. Children's programs became a very important part of television's growth. America was thriving and many people started families.

The most popular children's program during the 1940s and 1950s was a variety show with a Western theme called *Howdy Doody*. The show's star was a puppet named Howdy Doody.

Howdy Doody was filmed in front of a live studio audience made up of kids. Called the Peanut Gallery, the audience was part of the show. Buffalo Bob often spoke to the kids, involving them in the action.

There was also a clown named Clarabell and a host named Buffalo Bob Smith.

Children fell in love with the characters. They enjoyed the show so much that they rarely moved from their spots in front of the television once it began. Parents quickly recognized this as an opportunity to get things done around the house. If children were happily seated in front of the television, parents didn't have to chase them around or worry about what trouble they might be getting into. To this day, many parents use television as a way to entertain their kids when they need time to get chores done.

Generation TV

When *Howdy Doody* was on the air, children stopped what they were doing to watch the show. Advertisers sponsoring the show decided to use the show's power to sell products to kids. Buffalo Bob and the other characters would urge kids to tell their parents to buy different items. Kids begged their parents for these items and product sales soared.

Howdy Doody ran from 1947 to 1960. Its audience was the first generation raised on television. As the years passed, that generation grew up into the often rebellious young adults of the late 1960s and 1970s. Some critics of *Howdy Doody* blame the show for helping to create the troubled times. They claimed that parents had been less strict with their children, by just sitting them in front of the television instead of teaching them morals and values. Many people disagreed with the critics. They didn't believe the problems could simply be based on a TV show. Everyone could agree, however, that television was becoming an important force in American culture.

During the Vietnam War, American reporters were sent to Vietnam to cover the story. Shown here is journalist Walter Cronkite, reporting for CBS on February 28, 1968.

Changes on the Big Screen and Small Screen

The 1960s was a decade of social change for America. African Americans and women were fighting for civil rights, angry with the way they were treated by mainstream society. Americans were divided over the United States' involvement in the Vietnam War. A counterculture had developed, with hopes of spreading peace and love throughout the world.

TV News

On November 22, 1963, President John F. Kennedy was shot and killed in Dallas, Texas. Many Americans mourned his loss as if he had been a member of their own families. Television brought the country together, broadcasting constant news reports about the assassination. Every TV network covered the president's funeral. Americans grieved from their homes as they watched Jackie Kennedy and her children say goodbye to J.F.K.

With the Kennedy assassination, television further proved its important role in American culture. It became very clear that TV news reports recorded history as it happened. A TV reporter's presence at an event was a sign of the event's importance. The TV journalist became a symbol of the spread of trusted information. Television became America's primary source for news.

TV reporting played an important role in the coverage of the Vietnam War as well. Networks sent reporters and cameramen to Vietnam to report stories about the war. They captured images of bloody violence and heartbreaking tragedy. Reporters also covered the actions of anti-war protests throughout the

President John F. Kennedy was shot and killed on November 22, 1963, in Dallas, Texas. Two days later, Americans mourned along with the Kennedy family as they watched the president's memorial service on television.

United States. It was a very troubling time. The government wanted everyone to join together and support the war. As Americans watched television, however, more and more people became opposed to the war. Based on what they saw on television, many people even began to lose trust in the government.

The 1976 film, *Taxi Driver*, directed by Martin Scorsese, explored the dark and lonely feelings of a New York City cab driver. The movie was very popular and helped launch the careers of several successful actors, such as Jodie Foster (left) and Robert DeNiro (right).

Movie Blues

The growing mistrust of the government during the late 1960s and early 1970s led to Americans feeling isolated from one another. Many people were frustrated and angry. Many people felt disconnected from mainstream society. Hollywood responded with dark and unfriendly movies such as *Taxi*

Driver, Mean Streets, and *The Conversation.*
Their main characters were angry and different from the heroic characters people were
used to. Audiences connected with these
movies. Such films gave a voice to many
Americans' feelings.

Television Takes on Social Issues

A very brave sitcom of the 1970s changed
the future of TV programming—and America.
All in the Family, which first aired in 1971,
was one of the most important and influential
TV series in history. The show featured a
working-class family living in New York City.
The main character was Archie Bunker, a racist
man who was not afraid to let everyone know
how he felt. Bunker used hateful terms to
describe people of different races and religions.

While it may seem as though the program
excused this awful behavior, it actually did the
opposite. Archie's daughter and son-in-law
were open-minded and constantly criticized
Archie's behavior. *All in the Family* showed

Americans how ridiculous racism was, turning Archie into a symbol of what *not* to be. It also helped bring about a new generation of TV comedies that dealt with social issues. The show's impact sparked debates about what was appropriate subject matter for television. This once again proved television's important role in pop culture.

The Blockbuster Hits It Big

The American Dream offers the notion that anyone in America can earn lots of money and spend it on big, exciting purchases. Many Americans like bigger houses, bigger portions of food, bigger, faster cars, and bigger televisions. So, when Hollywood introduced the *bigger* movie, America accepted it with open arms.

In 1975, a young director named Steven Spielberg created a film about a killer shark that attacked unlucky swimmers in a small New England beach town. With its large-scale special effects and gory, bloody attack scenes, *Jaws* took the country by storm. This first big

Star Trek and Martin Luther King Jr.

The original *Star Trek* TV series aired on NBC from 1966-1969. During that time, African American actress Nichelle Nichols (top left) played Lieutenant Uhura on the show. When civil rights leader Martin Luther King Jr. heard that Nichols was considering leaving *Star Trek*, he asked her to stay. He knew she was a role model for future African American actresses.

film brought in more than $100 million. Americans flooded movie theaters again and again to witness the realistic-looking shark attacks. The blockbuster movie was born.

As successful as *Jaws* was, it didn't match the stunning impact of a movie released two years later. In 1977, *Star Wars*, written and directed by George Lucas, was released. Lucas created a science-fiction fantasy world in which a small yet brave band of people fought against an evil empire. The film was incredibly successful, bringing in over $400 million.

Blockbuster movies changed America and Hollywood. A movie was no longer simply a few hours of entertainment. The blockbuster crept into every part of American society. It was not only advertised on a much larger scale, but also marketed in the form of souvenirs. Toys, T-shirts, and even food products appeared, celebrating the characters and themes of the films. The blockbuster film is *so* big that it often seems unavoidable. Some critics claim that blockbusters have very little value.

The George Lucas blockbuster *Star Wars* was more than just a movie. It was so popular that it generated fan clubs, toys, and even conventions where fans got together, dressed as characters from the film.

They think the lack of complex story lines has "dumbed" down Americans by removing any artistic quality from films. However, the criticism has not stopped Hollywood from making these films. Producers and directors know that the blockbuster movie has found its home in American pop culture.

In 2001, *Lord of the Rings: The Fellowship of the Ring* was released.
The film, starring Sean Astin (left) and Elijah Wood (right), made over
$62 million in its first weekend of being shown in theaters.

Chapter

Modern Movies and Television

Movie Madness

Through the 1980s and 1990s, Hollywood continued to focus on making blockbuster movies, such as *E.T.: The Extra-Terrestrial*, *Batman*, *Terminator*, and *Jurassic Park*.

All were huge hits at the box office. Several independent filmmakers produced non-blockbusters, shunning Hollywood's obsession with big movies. These films were often aimed at adult moviegoers in big cities. Directors such as Spike Lee, Joel and Ethan Cohen, and Quentin Tarantino created smaller-budget

MTV started in 1981 as a cable network that aired music videos. Over the years, it has grown to become a trendsetting force in popular culture. Now, there are many different shows, such as *Total Request Live* and the annual *MTV Movie Awards* (shown here).

films which focused more on expressing artistic messages instead of making money.

Cable Enters the Picture

Television continued to grow, both technologically and in terms of show content. Cable networks such as the Home Box Office (HBO) and Showtime were created. Viewers paid an extra fee for these cable networks. These channels did not depend on advertising sponsors for funding. They had more freedom to push the boundaries of what could be shown on television. To compete with this new freedom, regular networks began to include programming with increased violence and more daring humor.

Going Digital

In the late 1990s and early 2000s, computers took on an important role in both television and movie production. New computer programs made it easier to create special effects. Computer-generated images (CGIs), such as those used in *Star Wars Episode I: The Phantom Menace* and *Star Wars Episode II: Attack of the Clones,* replaced most older effects styles. In the earlier *Star Wars* films, Yoda was a puppet controlled by strings. By the time *The Phantom Menace* and *Attack of the Clones* came out, Yoda was a CGI.

Buzz

When the Internet was developed in the late 1960s as a research network for the U.S. military, no one expected it to become a part of everyday American life. Members of the television and movie industry didn't expect it to become a way for audiences to make or break their work. Americans are constantly creating Web sites, often based on current movies and TV shows. Sometimes sites are created about a film before it is even released. Dedicated fans have found ways to get reports of a movie's production. They then create sites with comments, called buzz, to let other fans

Did You Know ?

MOVIE STUDIOS OFTEN ANONY-MOUSLY POST GOOD BUZZ ON THE INTERNET TO SWAY THE PUBLIC'S OPINION ABOUT THEIR FILMS!

On September 3, 2002, millions of viewers watched as Justin Guarini performed live on the reality show *American Idol*. At the end of the show, viewers were able to call in and vote for either Guarini or his competitor to win a record deal with a major recording company.

know what's going on. Whether it is good or bad, buzz spreads very quickly—and has the power to help or hurt a new film.

Keeping It Real

Reality shows took hold of American TV viewers in the late 1990s and early 2000s— and show no signs of letting go. Americans love reality programs such as *The Real World*, *Survivor*, and *American Idol*. Most regular TV shows offer representations, or symbols, of American life. Writers of these shows create characters and hope Americans will relate to them. Reality programs, however, simply show some Americans as they really are. Every new TV season brings reality shows that are more and more outrageous.

Movies and television are at the heart of American culture. As Americans watch characters on the big and small screens, they see examples of American life. The characters are so real that they feel like friends and family members. They both reflect and help shape the way Americans exist. For many decades, movies and television have been an important part of American culture. Each has celebrated and helped to define what it means to be American—and will do so for many years to come. Whether it's by recording history or shaping it, television and movies will always be at the heart of American pop culture.

Successful movies and TV shows present characters that audiences can relate to. In the very best ones, the characters become our friends. Shown here is the cast of the popular NBC sitcom *Friends*.

New Words

assassination (uh-sass-uh-**nay**-shun) the murder of someone who is important or well known, such as the president

broadcast (**brawd**-kast) to send out a program on television or radio; a television or radio program

encoded (en-**kode**-did) converted from one system of communication into another

generation (jen-uh-**ray**-shuhn) all the people born around the same time

images (**im**-ij-ez) representations such as pictures or statues

isolated (**eye**-suh-lay-tid) kept separate

journalist (**jur**-nuhl-ist) someone who collects information and writes articles for newspapers, television, or radio

new words

mainstream (**mayn**-streem) the most common direction or trend of a movement

passionate (**pash**-uh-nit) having or showing very strong feelings

portrayal (por-**tray**-uhl) an acted part in a play or movie

projector (pruh-**jek**-tur) a machine that shows slides or movies on a screen

record (ri-**kord**) to tape or write down information so it can be kept

relate (ri-**late**) to feel connected to something

sitcom (**sit**-kom) short for situation comedy, a humorous television program that features the same group of characters each week

Hasday, Judy L. *Extraordinary People in the Movies.* Danbury, CT: Children's Press, 2003.

Mattern, Joanne. *Television: Window to the World.* New York: The Rosen Publishing Group, Inc., 2003.

O'Brien, Lisa. *Lights, Camera, Action!: Making Movies and TV from the Inside Out.* Toronto, Ontario, Canada: Owl Books, 1998.

Wordsworth, Louise. *Film and Television.* Orlando, FL: Raintree/Steck Vaughn, 1998.

Resources

Organizations

The American Film Institute
2021 North Western Avenue
Los Angeles, CA 90027
(323) 856-7600
www.afi.com

**The Museum of Television and Radio
in Los Angeles**
465 North Beverly Drive
Beverly Hills, CA 90210
(310) 786-1000
www.mtr.org

Resources

Web Sites

Internet Movie Database

www.imdb.com

This Web site offers information on practically every movie and television program ever produced in America. The site allows searches by people or title. It also has links to other movie and television Web sites.

Academy of Television Arts and Sciences

www.emmys.com

This is the offical Web site of the Academy of Television Arts and Sciences. It offers articles and interviews with television program creators and actors.

Academy of Motion Picture Arts and Sciences

www.oscars.org

This is the offical Web site of the Academy of Motion Picture Arts and Sciences. It offers a list of every person who has ever won an Oscar.

InDex

InDex

About the Author

Philip Abraham is a freelance writer.
He has a Bachelor of Arts degree in Film
Production. He has written many books for
children and young adults.